W9-BXE-889

A Taste of Culture

Foods of Germany

Barbara Sheen

KIDHAVEN PRESS
An imprint of Thomson Gale, a part of The Thomson Corporation

THOMSON
─────✦─────™
GALE

Detroit • New York • San Francisco • New Haven, Conn. • Waterville, Maine • London

THOMSON

★

GALE

™

© 2007 by KidHaven Press. KidHaven Press is an imprint of The Gale Group, Inc.,
a division of Thomson Learning, Inc.

KidHaven™ and Thomson Learning™ are trademarks used herein under license.

For more information, contact
KidHaven Press
27500 Drake Rd.
Farmington Hills, MI 48331-3535
Or you can visit our Internet site at http://www.gale.com

Every effort has been made to trace the owners of copyrighted material.

LIBRARY OF CONGRESS CATALOGING-IN-PUBLICATION DATA

Sheen, Barbara.
    Foods of Germany / by Barbara Sheen.
        p. cm. — (A taste of culture)
Includes bibliographical references.
ISBN-13: 978-0-7377-3554-3 (hardcover : alk. paper)
ISBN-10: 0-7377-3554-6 (hardcover : alk. paper)
1.   Cookery, German—Juvenile literature.   I. Title.
TX721.S53 2006
641.5'943—dc22

                                                                2006018667

Printed in the United States of America

Contents

1

Three Important Ingredients

When people think of German food, three ingredients usually come to mind. They are pork, cabbage, and potatoes. These foods thrive here. And German cooks use them in hundreds of delicious dishes.

Most Germans love meat, and pork is far and away the national favorite. Germany is a small country. Much of the land is wooded or mountainous. The terrain is poorly suited to the large-scale raising of cattle and sheep. These animals do best in large pastures. Pigs, on the other hand, prosper on small German farms. That is probably why more than half of all the meat consumed in Germany is pork.

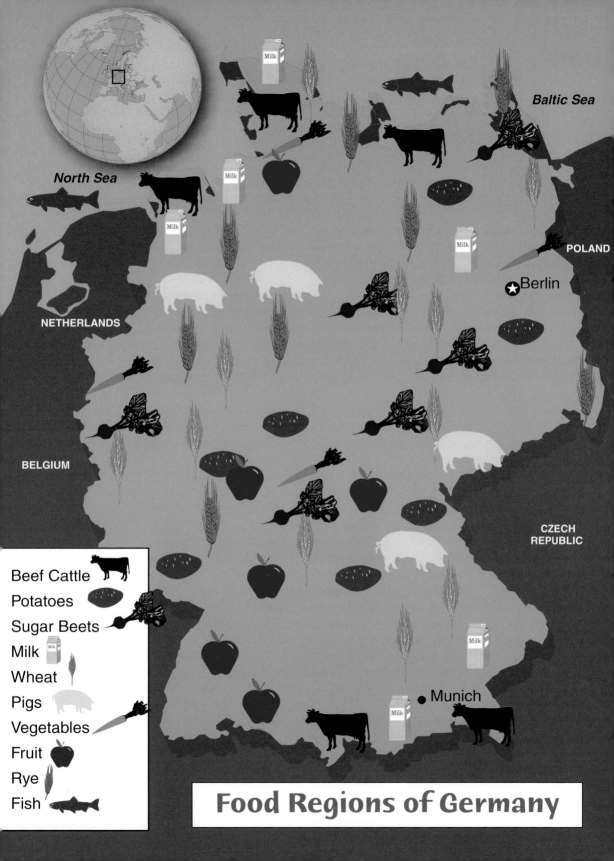

Food Regions of Germany

Many Uses

Germans have been eating pork for hundreds of years. Early Germans hunted boars, a type of wild pig, which they cooked on a spit over an open fire. The meat was such an essential part of the ancient German diet that a 2,000-year-old mosaic floor in the city of Cologne depicts a wild boar roast.

Succulent pork with apples is one of the many ways pig meat is prepared in Germany.

As Germans began raising pigs, cooks developed hundreds of ways to use every part of the animal. Pig fat is used to make lard for frying. The stomach is stuffed with pork cubes, potatoes, and spices. And popular specialties include pork chops, knuckles, feet, ribs, head, and tongue.

Creative German chefs add pig meat to soups and stews, stuff it in dumplings, and grind it for sausages, meat loaf, and pork patties. In fact, the American hamburger comes from German pork patties, which were first served in the city of Hamburg in 1903. Pork roast, which is made from the pig's backside, is traditionally served for Sunday dinner. Maria Swaringen, who grew up in Germany, recalls: "I still remember smelling the delightful aroma of a pork roast every Sunday as I walked home from church . . . and passed one house after another."[1]

Cured Meat

If all these uses are not enough, German chefs **cure** pork by salting and smoking it to make bacon and ham. This practice started more than 1,000 years ago as a way to preserve the meat.

Germans make many different types of ham, including Westphalian ham, which many people say is the best-tasting ham in the world. It is made from the hind legs of free-roaming pigs that live in the Westphalia Forest of northern Germany. The pigs are fed a special diet of acorns, which fattens them and makes their meat moist and tasty. To cure the meat, it is hand rubbed with salt and sugar. This removes almost all the moisture from it, which prevents it from spoiling. Then the meat is slowly smoked over a fragrant beech wood fire for at least a month.

The Cabbage Queen

Cabbage is so beloved in Germany that the village of Wohrden holds a yearly cabbage festival. Young women compete in a beauty contest for the title of Cabbage Queen.

The queen rides through the town in a carriage surrounded by hundreds of heads of cabbage. When she reaches the town square, the citizens build a tall pyramid out of the cabbages. A huge feast follows in which every dish is made with cabbage.

Cabbage is one of Germany's most popular vegetables.

A butcher inspects racks of ham before they are shipped to a smokehouse to be cured.

Germans have been making Westphalian ham in this manner since the 1100s. The resulting ham has a delicate smoky taste and smell. Germans love to slice it paper-thin and eat it on crusty pumpernickel bread slathered with butter. This meal is so beloved in Germany that a 15th-century German cathedral window depicts Jesus Christ and his disciples eating West-phalian ham on black bread at the Last Supper.

The Most Popular Vegetable

Pork is almost always accompanied by cabbage, the most popular vegetable in Germany. Wild cabbage grows well in Germany's cool, wet climate. Germans grow seventeen different varieties of cabbage. The varieties come in three colors—red, green, and white.

Germans have many different ways of preparing cabbage. They simmer it with carrots and mushrooms, mash it with potatoes, brown it with onions and bacon, or braise it with sliced apples. They also turn it into cabbage soup or cabbage pudding, stuff it with ground pork, add it to stews and casseroles, or shred it for slaw. "There is no vegetable more popular than cabbage throughout Germany," explains German chef Marianna Olszewska Heberle. "And anyone who thinks otherwise may be affectionately called a *kohlkopf* [cole-cuf] . . . a cabbage head,"[2] she jokes.

The most popular way Germans use cabbage is to pickle it for **sauerkraut** (sow-er-krout). Sauerkraut originated 2,300 years ago in ancient China as a way to preserve cabbage. It was brought to Germany in the 1200s by the invading army of Genghis Khan. The German people loved the taste and the fact that pickling cabbage kept the fragile vegetable from spoiling.

Germans make sauerkraut by layering finely shredded cabbage with salt in a wooden barrel. The salt ferments the cabbage, converting the vegetable's natural juice into a sharp tangy liquid that gives sauerkraut its special flavor. In the past, sauerkraut was always homemade. Although some modern Germans still make their own sauerkraut, freshly made sauerkraut is available in butcher shops throughout the nation.

Germans eat about 3.75 pounds (1.70kg) of sauerkraut per person every year. They use sauerkraut in almost everything. It is the main ingredient in relishes, soups, casseroles, salads, and vegetable dishes. It is even used in cakes. Chef Katy Shaw Nelson explains: "The eating of this flavorful food is almost a way of life—it seems as if sauerkraut or some variation has appeared on just about every German plate for centuries."[3]

A plate of stuffed cabbage provides comfort at mealtime.

Sauerkraut with Apples

This is a tasty side dish. If you want the sauerkraut to taste less sour, wash and drain it.

Ingredients:

1 large tart apple, cored and chopped
1 teaspoon lemon juice
1 large carrot, peeled and shredded
1 teaspoon sugar
1 pound sauerkraut
salt and pepper to taste

Instructions:

1. Put the chopped apple in a bowl. Sprinkle the lemon juice over the apple to keep it from turning brown.
2. Add the carrot, sugar, sauerkraut, salt, and pepper and mix well.
3. Cover the bowl and refrigerate for at least one hour. Serve cold.

Makes 4 to 6 servings.

A Life Saver

Potatoes are another important part of every German's diet. But this was not always the case. Potatoes came from South America. They were brought to Europe by 16th-century Spanish mariners. When German peasants first tasted the vegetable, which they ate raw and unpeeled, they became sick. As a result, potatoes were deemed unfit for humans until the 1600s. At that time King Frederick the Great ordered the German people to plant and eat the vegetable to avoid hunger during food shortages, which were common then. To ensure obedience, Frederick threatened to cut off the ears of anyone who refused to eat the tubers.

Potatoes flourished in Germany's soil and climate, saving many people from starving in the 1600s and

Sauerkraut and Health

Sauerkraut is very nutritious. It is rich in vitamins A, thiamin, riboflavin, and C and the minerals iron, and potassium. It also is loaded with fiber and is fat free.

Sauerkraut appears to have many health benefits. Scientists say that sauerkraut contains chemicals that may prevent cancer growth. It also contains helpful bacteria that may destroy salmonella, harmful bacteria that cause food poisoning. Not only that, scientists believe that the vegetable contains chemicals that kill the virus that causes the bird flu.

Potatoes

1700s and once again during World War II. "During and after WWII everyone was out in the fields looking for potatoes,"[4] recalls Swaringen.

Over time, potatoes became a staple of the German diet. Today German farmers grow more than 700 different varieties, and each German eats about 165 pounds (75kg) of the tuber every year.

Germans use potatoes in hundreds of dishes. They combine mashed potatoes and stewed apples to make a popular dish known as Heaven and Earth. They stuff dumplings with potatoes, thicken soups and stews with them, and fill casseroles with them. They also make them into crispy potato pancakes, which they serve topped with fresh applesauce, pickled red cabbage, or sour cream. And they mix them with vinegar, bacon, and onions to make dozens of different hot and cold potato salads.

Potato Salad

Germans love potato salad. This is a simple potato salad recipe.

Ingredients:
6 medium potatoes, peeled and cut into thick slices
1 small onion, peeled and chopped
3 tablespoons red wine vinegar
3 tablespoons vegetable oil
1 teaspoon sugar
1 tablespoon chopped dill
1 tablespoon bacon bits
salt and pepper to taste

Instructions:
1. Cook potatoes in a pot filled with enough water to completely cover the potatoes. Cook until the potatoes are soft, about 15 minutes. Drain cooked potatoes.
2. Put the drained potatoes in a large bowl. Add the bacon bits.
3. Combine the rest of the ingredients in a separate bowl. Pour this mixture over the potatoes and stir.
4. Cover and put in the refrigerator for at least one hour. Serve cold.

Makes 4 to 6 servings.

Depending on the other ingredients, German potato salads can be quite simple. Or they can contain a wide range of ingredients, including sausage, ham, hard-boiled eggs, cheese, pickles, apples, mustard, or pickled herring. But no matter what other ingredients are used, the main one is potato. The other ingredients only help bring out its flavor. Nan, whose family is German, explains that German potato salad "has a wonderful bacon flavor, but the potato is the star."[5]

Potatoes, cabbage, and pork are indeed the stars of German cooking. These three ingredients give German food its unique flavor. German **cuisine** would not be the same without them.

Chapter

2

Satisfying Hearty Appetites

Germans love to eat. "A full belly," a German proverb says, "is more precious than silver or gold."[6] Favorite dishes like **schnitzel** (shnit-sel), **sauerbraten** (zow-er-brah-ten), and dumplings and noodles satisfy hearty appetites. At the same time, they warm Germans' spirits on chilly, damp days, which are common much of the year.

Pounded and Fried

Schnitzel is the German word for a boneless slice of veal, pork, or chicken that is pounded flat, breaded, and panfried until golden. It is similar to American chicken-fried steak.

Cooking meat in this manner began in the Middle Ages. Historians have records of schnitzel being served in Germany as early as the 1000s. Traditionally the meat is pounded with a wooden mallet, which not only flattens the meat but also makes it tender. Then it is dipped in egg and rolled in flour and bread crumbs. It is fried in butter until the meat is moist and tender and the breading is crisp, golden brown, and butter flavored.

Serving Schnitzel

Schnitzel is usually served with a slice of lemon. Sauerkraut and mashed potatoes sprinkled with melted butter and bread crumbs often accompany it. Sometimes the meat is topped with a mushroom or cream sauce. Or the meat may be crowned with fried eggs and anchovies. This is known as Holstein schnitzel, named after Baron Friedrich von Holstein. According to German legend, this 18th-century German diplomat worked nonstop. He thought taking a break to eat breakfast and lunch wasted time. So his cook found a way to combine the two meals into one by creating Holstein schnitzel. The eggs and anchovies were the baron's breakfast, and the schnitzel was his lunch.

Veal is the most commonly used meat for schnitzel. Veal schnitzel is known as **wiener schnitzel** (vee-ner shnit-sel). John, who lived in Germany for one year, says it is one of his favorite foods. "It is so delicious," he says. "Thinking about it makes my mouth water. The meat is soft and succulent and the breading has to be the best part. It is flaky, crusty, and just yummy."[7]

Delicious sauerbraten combines crumbled gingersnap cookies and vinegar to create sweet and sour flavors.

Schnitzel

This recipe also works with boneless chicken breasts or pork cutlets.

Ingredients:
4 veal cutlets, about 1/4-inch thick
1 large egg
1 cup bread crumbs
1 teaspoon each salt and pepper
2 tablespoons butter or margarine for frying

Instructions:

1. Put the meat between two sheets of plastic wrap. Pound the meat lightly with a meat mallet to flatten it.
2. Beat the egg in a large shallow bowl. Place the bread crumbs in another large shallow bowl.
3. Remove the plastic wrap from the meat. Sprinkle the meat with salt and pepper.
4. Dip both sides of the meat into the egg and then into the bread crumbs, coating the meat. Do this with each slice of meat.
5. Heat the butter or margarine in a frying pan over medium heat. Add the meat and fry about four minutes on each side. The breading should be golden and the meat white.
6. Serve with a slice of lemon and/or a fried egg on top.

Makes 4 servings.

Sweet and Sour

Sauerbraten, which means "sour roast," is another tasty dish that Germans love. It is usually made from beef, which is marinated in a tangy sauce that gives it a wonderful sweet-and-sour flavor.

Pancakes

Pancakes are another popular German food, and potato pancakes are among everyone's favorites. Germans make potato pancakes either from freshly grated potatoes or from leftover potatoes, which they mash. An egg, grated onion, and flour are added to the potatoes. The mixture is formed into patties, which are fried until brown and crisp.

Germans eat potato pancakes as an accompaniment to any meal, including breakfast. When they are topped with stew or a thick mushroom sauce, they are the main course.

The crispy treats are also a common snack. It is not unusual to see German children munching on potato pancakes as they play in the street.

Crispy potato pancakes can be eaten as a snack or a main course.

To make sauerbraten, German cooks marinate a beef roast in a mixture of vinegar, cloves, bay leaves, peppercorns, and onion for up to a week. The vinegar tenderizes the beef, and the spices give it a wonderful flavor and smell. The roast is then cooked in the marinade. Crumbled gingersnap cookies are often added to the pan juices to sweeten and thicken the gravy.

Germans have been eating sauerbraten for centuries. Historians say that King **Charlemagne** (Shar-le-main), of Germany, invented the dish as a way of making tough cuts of beef easier to eat.

Sauerbraten is often served with applesauce, red cabbage, and potato pancakes, noodles, or dumplings. It has a robust meaty taste. According to an expert at the German embassy in Washington D.C., "Sauerbraten is one of the best-known German dishes. After days of marinating, the meat is infused with many flavors and becomes quite tender—perfect for a cozy winter meal."[8]

Dumplings and Noodles

Sauerbraten and schnitzel are likely to be served with dumplings or noodles, hearty starches that are found at almost every meal. "What spaghetti and pasta are to Italy, what potatoes are to Ireland, what pierogies are to Poland, noodles and dumplings are to Germany,"[9] explains Olszewska Heberle.

Germans make a wide variety of noodles. Squiggly egg noodles known as **spaetzle** (shpehtz-el) are among the most popular. These tasty noodles are thin and tiny. As a

Raw noodles cook in a pot of boiling water after they are pushed through the holes of a spaetzle maker.

matter of fact, the word *spaetzle* means "skinny little sparrow" in German.

The dough is made from flour, water, eggs, salt, and sometimes nutmeg. Traditionally, a special tool known as a spaetzle maker is used to shape the noodles. It is a grater with very large holes. The dough is pushed through the holes into a pot of boiling water. In a matter of minutes, the noodles float to the surface, which means they are done. In the past almost every German bride was

This hearty meal includes thick gravy slathered over roast beef and a large dumpling.

given a spaetzle maker as a wedding gift. According to German legend, the number of dough droppings that fell into the pot when she first used the device predicted how many children she would have in the future.

And because spaetzle making is not difficult, these same children were often assigned the job of pushing the dough through the grater. Today, when many families are too busy to make their own spaetzle, ready-made fresh and dried spaetzle is sold in supermarkets.

Whether store-bought or homemade, spaetzle tastes rich and delicious. It is often served right from the pot tossed with butter. Or cooked spaetzle is fried with onions, mushrooms, and bacon or minced liver. But no matter what it is cooked with, spaetzle is creamy, buttery, and filling. Janet, who cooks spaetzle for her family, explains: "During my years living in Germany I learned many good dishes and this is one of my family's favorite. It is especially good on those cool evenings when you want some comfort food."[10]

Waste Not

Dumplings are another traditional German favorite. Besides being delicious, they give thrifty cooks a way to use stale bread and other leftovers. Germans make hundreds of different dumplings. Their ingredients, shape, and size are as varied as the people who make them.

Dumpling dough often consists of stale bread soaked in milk or leftover mashed potatoes mixed with water,

Bread Dumplings

This is a good way to use old bread.

Ingredients:
1 loaf French bread or white bread
1 cup warm milk
2 tablespoons melted butter
¼ teaspoon salt
2 eggs
2 tablespoons chopped parsley
pinch of pepper and nutmeg
3 tablespoons flour

Instructions:
1. Break the bread into small pieces and put in a large bowl. Pour the milk, melted butter, and salt over the bread.
2. Add the other ingredients and mix well. It should form a stiff batter.
3. Form the batter into egg-size balls.
4. Bring a large pot of water to a boil. Drop the dumplings in the boiling water. Lower the heat and cook uncovered about fifteen minutes. The dumplings are done when they float to the top.

Makes 4 servings.

eggs, and flour. But some dumplings are made with yeast dough. Ingredients such as ground minced liver and onions that have been fried in butter are added to the dough to make liver dumplings. This may not sound appealing to some Americans, but they are among the most well-liked dumplings in Germany. Swaringen explains: "I know for many people liver dumplings sound just awful,

German Meals

Germans usually eat three meals a day. Muesli and milk is a typical breakfast. Muesli is a cereal made of raw and toasted grains such as wheat, oats, and wheat germ mixed with nuts, dried fruits, and seeds. Rolls spread with honey, jam, chocolate, or cheese are also popular.

Lunch is the largest meal of the day. It is served around noon and is almost always a hot meal. It usually includes soup, meat, potatoes, cabbage or sauerkraut, and gravy. A sweet dessert follows.

Dinner is a light meal. It is eaten between six and seven o'clock and is frequently a cold meal. Thinly sliced ham and other cold cuts, a variety of cheeses, multigrain bread, and fresh vegetables are typical dinner fare. The different food items are served on a wooden tray or board, and everyone helps him- or herself.

Germans enjoy tasty treats during an outdoor meal.

Satisfying Hearty Appetites 27

let alone would they want to eat them; but believe me, they are absolutely delicious."[11]

Other ground meats are also popular fillings, as are different fruits, such as plums, apples, or cherries sweetened with sugar. Once the filling is selected it can be mixed right into the dough, which is formed into little balls. Or the filling is placed in the center of little dough squares that are folded over like tiny envelopes. The dumplings are then cooked in boiling water. They are ready in only a few minutes.

Savory dumplings accompany almost everything. They are often topped with rich mushroom gravy. They are also used in soups and stews. Hot or cold sweet dumplings are a popular dessert and a common warm weather meal. They may be bathed in fruit syrup or vanilla sauce, or served like cereal, with milk. Author John T. Dickman fondly remembers his German mother's apple dumplings: "Mom's were spirals of biscuit-like dough embracing an apple-sugar-cinnamon filling." He explains that these dumplings "claim a . . . secure hold on the memories of the past."[12]

The taste of delicious dishes like rich sweet-and-savory dumplings, buttery spaetzle, zesty sauerbraten, and crispy schnitzel are indeed memorable. These tasty foods satisfy even the heartiest appetites. It is no wonder they are German favorites.

chapter 3

Sandwiches and Sweets

Snacking is an important part of German life. Workers typically enjoy crusty breads, savory sausages, and delicious sandwiches during a mid-morning **brotzeit** (broot-zite), or bread break. Late afternoon get-togethers known as **coffee klatsches** (klatches) are the perfect time for friends to visit over pastries.

Bread-Breaking Time

Germans work hard. But every morning around ten o'clock, they like to stop what they are doing for a bread break. This often consists of a roll or thick slab of bread slathered with sweet butter. Or it might be an open-faced sandwich made with a slice of rye bread topped

Germans take a break from their busy day to enjoy coffee.

with ham and cheese. The more than 200 varieties of German breads give snackers many, many choices.

German breads can be long or short, round or square, white, tan, brown, or almost black. There are whole-wheat breads, rye breads, pumpernickel breads, sweet raisin breads, breads dotted with sunflower or pumpkin seeds, soft rolls, hard rolls, and rolls coated with cheese. No matter the type though, all German breads are baked fresh daily without artificial flavorings or preservatives. Germans would have it no other way.

Pretzels

Pretzels—fresh soft yeast breads sprinkled with salt—are one of the most popular of all German bread snacks. German folklore says that the knot-shaped treats were invented by a 7th-century monk who twisted together scraps of dough to form a roll that looked like hands crossed in prayer. The monk used the salty treats as rewards for children who memorized their prayers.

Pretzels became popular throughout Germany. Traveling pretzel vendors carrying the rolls on long poles or wearing them hanging from strings around their necks became a common sight.

Today pretzels are sold almost everywhere. Unlike hard, crisp American pretzels, German pretzels are soft and crusty. They taste great covered with spicy mustard or served with a piece of cheese or sausage, which is just the way Germans like to eat them.

Pretzels have been a popular snack in Germany for centuries.

Open-Faced Sandwiches

Open-faced sandwiches are a favorite German snack. They are made with only one slice of bread and are eaten with a knife and fork. You can use any toppings you prefer.

Ingredients
4 slices pumpernickel bread
2 tablespoons butter, room temperature
4 slices Bavarian or Emmentaler Swiss cheese (or substitute any Swiss cheese)
4 slices Black Forest ham (or substitute any other ham or bologna)
4 slices sour pickle

Instructions:
1. Butter each slice of bread.
2. Put a slice of meat and cheese on each slice of bread. Serve with a pickle slice on the side.

Makes 4 servings.

Bread is so important to Germans that bakers must be licensed, which requires years of training. Spanking clean, deliciously scented bakeries are found all over Germany. And nothing is prepackaged. Customers can purchase anything from one freshly sliced piece of bread to a giant loaf. The baker aims to please. "I miss going down to the corner bakery and picking up **brochen** (brot-chen) [rolls]," explains Patty, who lived in Germany. "My mouth still waters at the prospect of . . . pumpkin seed rolls. Oh! They were so good!"[13]

Hundreds of Sausages

According to most Germans, nothing tastes better with fresh bread or rolls than **wurst** (vurst), the German word for sausage. Sausages slathered with sweet or hot mustard and eaten with crusty bread may very well be the most popular snack in Germany. In the city of Munich alone, hungry Germans eat 100,000 **weisswursts** (vice-vursts), a type of veal sausage, each and every day.

Germans make 1,700 different kinds of sausages, which are sold everywhere. "There are snack stands or

Two women prepare wursts that will be sold in their restaurant.

stand-up snack bars located on busy shopping streets, in parking lots, train stations, and markets where sausages of all kinds are dispensed—grilled, roasted, or boiled in all shapes and sizes,"[14] reports Olszewska Heberle.

People have been making sausages since the start of recorded history. Germans learned how to make the tasty links from the ancient Romans who occupied Germany from 13 B.C. to A.D. 457. At that time, making sausages provided people with a way to preserve meat. It also allowed them a way to make use of animal parts that might otherwise go to waste.

Traditionally, sausages are made by stuffing finely ground meat, herbs, and spices inside a casing made from the intestines of sheep, pigs, or cattle. The salt and spices preserve the meat, which is often cooked and/or smoked before it is placed in the casing. Although casings made from animal intestines are still used, artificial casings are common today.

Stuffed inside the sausage casing are any number of fillings. They come in varying colors based on the type of meat used. They can be hard or soft depending on how the meat is prepared. And, depending on which seasonings are added, they can be salty, spicy, or sweet.

A Variety of Flavors

The varieties are seemingly endless. There are savory bratwurst made with pork, beef, nutmeg, pepper, and caraway seeds; short, fat, pink bockwurst; and crunchy pork and garlic knackwurst. There are 60 varieties of liv-

Wurst can be made spicy, salty, or sweet. Here it is served with sauerkraut and potato salad.

erwurst made from pork or calf's liver, which is ground with onions or mushrooms or even anchovies. There is spicy curry-flavored currywurst and black blood sausage made from a mix of ground pork and fresh pig's blood. And there is the **frankfurter** (frahnk-foorter), which is named for the city of Frankfurt where they were invented. It is also known as the American hot dog.

German sausages are eaten cold or hot. Some varieties come from the store precooked and ready to eat. Others are raw and in need of cooking. Whether eaten cold with a slice of hard cheese, boiled in beer, or buried under a mountain of sauerkraut, these meaty links are bound to

Shopping in Germany

Germany has many modern supermarkets, but food shopping in Germany is different than in the United States. Supermarket shoppers must pay a few cents for the use of a shopping cart. They must weigh their own produce too, since supermarket clerks do not provide this service.

Shoppers can also buy food in department stores. One department store in Berlin devotes an entire floor to luxury food items such as seafood, meats, and cheeses. The store also has a food court with an enormous selection of cakes, tortes, and chocolates just waiting for hungry shoppers.

There are also many small specialty stores throughout Germany, such as butcher shops, fish stores, delicatessens that sell smoked meats and sausage, fruit and vegetable markets, chocolate shops, and bakeries. But no matter where Germans shop, all food stores are closed on Sunday. All shoppers must bring their own grocery bags. Many Germans use reusable cloth grocery sacks in order to protect the environment.

Shoppers explore an abundance of produce at an outdoor market.

please. A German **wurstmacher** (vurst-mock-er), or sausage maker, will make sure of that. They take great pride in their creations. All sausages are made with the utmost of care. German laws regulate sausage production, ensuring that no fillers or additives are used. This is not surprising, since sausages are more than just a food in Germany. They are a treasured part of German life. "They are dearly beloved by most people, perhaps even held in awe and reverence,"[15] explains author Myra Waldo.

Coffee and Cake

When afternoon rolls around, Germans try to make time for a sweet ritual known as a coffee klatsch. This is a time for friends to gather over a cup of coffee and a rich piece of pastry.

German pastries are world famous and are available in seemingly endless varieties. There are fancy multilayered treats, which Germans call **torten** (tort-en), and **kuchen** (koo-ken), single-layered cakes. Among the most popular kuchens are coffee cakes. They are made with yeast dough, which gives them a breadlike texture. They are often topped with slices of fresh peaches or apples and a crunchy layer of sweet crumbs made from flour, butter, and vanilla sugar. The vanilla sugar is made by combining sugar and vanilla beans. Sometimes fresh whipped cream or slivered chocolate is added. Such cakes are considered simple, everyday cakes and can be found in most bakeries, cafés, and German kitchens.

Kuchen are single-layered cakes that come in many delicious flavors, including blueberry (pictured).

Fruit is also featured in many other German cakes. Germans love to use whatever fruit is in season in their baking. Many of these cakes are similar to American pies in that rolled dough, rather than a pourable batter, is used. Fresh-cut apple, plum, or peach slices are arranged on the dough and topped with vanilla sugar, powdered sugar, fruit preserves, or slivered almonds. These cakes are sweet, but not too sweet, with a fresh aroma.

German chocolate cakes are richer and sweeter than the fruit cakes. There are dozens of delicious varieties.

Black Forest cake is among the most famous. It is a very rich, multilayered dark chocolate torte that originated in the 1500s in the Black Forest region of southern Germany. Because the recipe

Bakers sell bread and pastries of all sorts from their large display cases.

Easy Black Forest Cake

This recipe uses a cake mix and is not difficult to make.

Ingredients:
1 devil's food cake mix
1 20-ounce can cherry pie filling
1 8-ounce container whipped cream topping
12 maraschino cherries

Instructions:
1. Prepare the cake batter following the package directions. Pour the batter into two round cake pans sprayed with nonstick spray. Bake and let cakes cool.
2. Invert one cake onto a plate. Spread the cherry pie filling on top.
3. Carefully put the other cake on top of the filling. Spread the whipped cream over the top and sides of the cake. Decorate the top with the cherries.

Makes 8 to 12 servings.

calls for a lot of sugar, which was very expensive at that time, only German royalty ate it. When the price of sugar decreased in the 1700s, it became popular with everyone.

Black Forest cake is a chocolate lover's dream. It consists of several layers of moist chocolate cake, fresh whipped cream, and juicy cherries. The whole thing is covered with whipped cream frosting and decorated with long-stemmed cherries. Delicate chocolate curls, which are made by rubbing a chocolate square with a potato peeler, are the final touch.

The result is a divinely rich cake that looks as wonderful as it tastes. A baker at Grandma's Marketplace, a bakery that specializes in German sweets, agrees: "This fabulous chocolate classic . . . is a sheer delight to the senses—it is truly delicious and enchanting,"[16]

With tasty sweets like Black Forest cake, and savory treats like sausages served with fresh baked breads and rolls, it is no wonder Germans love to snack. These mouthwatering treats are hard to resist.

Holiday Treats

Holidays are celebrated in Germany with an assortment of sweets. Many of these traditional treats have been a part of German life for centuries.

A Special Time

Christmas is a special time of year in Germany. Baking Christmas cookies is a holiday tradition. During the month leading up to Christmas, families get together to make and decorate a variety of holiday cookies. Platters loaded with homemade cookies are the centerpieces of afternoon coffee klatsches. They are also popular holiday gifts.

Rich, soft butter cookies in the shape of Christmas trees, crunchy cinnamon stars, and church-bell-shaped yeast cookies are favorites. Beautifully decorated sugar cookies known as **springerles** (shpring-uhr-lees) also have a special place on the cookie plate.

Germans have been making springerles since the 1400s. They are white sugar cookies flavored with anise, a licorice-like spice. What makes springerles special is that

An intricately carved rolling pin presses a beautiful design into springerle dough.

A young boy makes cookies, a Christmas tradition in Germany.

each cookie is imprinted with an elaborate design. The design is made with a carved rolling pin or a wooden stamp similar to a printing stamp.

Designs include biblical scenes, floral and animal pictures, and Christmas designs. German bakers paint the designs with food coloring, turning them into works of art that can be eaten or used as Christmas tree ornaments.

Springerles have a crunchy texture that makes them perfect for dunking. They taste best if stored in an airtight container for at least a week before they are eaten. This removes moisture and makes them crisper. An apple slice placed in the container keeps the cookies from getting too hard. Horst, whose family is German, recalls: "Mother . . . was sure to send me these cookies every Christmas. They are to be 'dunked' in coffee and are addictive!"[17]

Many Shapes

Lebkuchen (layb-koo-ken), or gingerbread, is almost always found on the cookie platter. Germans have been making it for hundreds of years.

Gingerbread came from honey cake. During the Middle Ages Germans baked honey cakes as an offering to spirits at Christmas time. Once spices from Asia became available, German monks added ginger to the honey cake and gingerbread was born.

Soft, moist German gingerbread comes in many forms, from cakes and loaves to cookies. Gingerbread cookies in the shape of human figures and decorated with dried fruits, nuts, and candies became popular in the 1600s. But gingerbread people are not the only shape you can find in Germany. Gingerbread cookies are made to look like stars, bells, wreathes, Christmas stockings, and angels. These may be quite plain or richly decorated with colored icing.

Gingerbread People

These cookies are fun to make. Decorate them with raisins, candies, and frosting.

Ingredients:
2½ cups all-purpose unbleached flour
¼ teaspoon each ground nutmeg, ground cloves
1 teaspoon cinnamon
1 teaspoon ground ginger
1 teaspoon salt
1 teaspoon baking soda
¾ cup soft margarine or butter
½ cup brown sugar
1 egg
½ cup molasses

Instructions:

1. Combine the flour, spices, and baking soda in a large bowl.
2. In a separate bowl mix the margarine or butter and sugar. Add the egg and molasses. Mix well.
3. Add the wet ingredients to the flour mixture and mix well.
4. Divide the dough in half. Wrap each in plastic wrap and refrigerate for one to two hours.
5. Preheat oven to 350°F. Put the dough on a floured surface and roll out until it is about 1/8- to 1/4-inch thick. Use cookie cutters to cut out the cookies.
6. Transfer the cookies to a cookie sheet sprayed with nonstick spray, spacing the cookies at least 1 inch apart.
7. Bake cookies until firm, about ten to twelve minutes. Allow cookies to cool before decorating.

Perhaps the most famous gingerbread creation is the gingerbread house. It was inspired by German authors the Brothers Grimm and their story *Hansel and Gretel*. A German baker created the first gingerbread house in the early 1800s. Like the witch's cottage in the fairy tale, it was decorated with gumdrops and candy canes, another German invention.

Making gingerbread houses became a German holiday tradition, which spread to the United States. The houses, along with gingerbread cookies, decorate homes and shops throughout Germany at Christmas. Their presence reminds Germans that it is Christmas time. Kerstin, whose family is German, explains: "My mother grew up near Munich. . . . Every year for Christmas, her godfather would send her a big box of Lebkuchen, which my brother and I would devour by New Years. We both felt that when Uncle Norbert's cookies came, Christmas had officially started."[18]

Life-Size Gingerbread

In the past, schoolchildren in the German city of Frankfurt would get together and bake a gingerbread person that was as large as their teacher. The children gave the life-size cookie to the teacher as a Christmas present, which they would all eat as part of their in-school Christmas celebration.

Stollen

Stollen (shtoh-luhn) is another traditional Christmas sweet. German Christmas would not be the same without it. This yeast cake, filled with candied fruit and nuts, is similar to fruitcake. But to Germans it is more than just a rich cake. Its tapered, plump, oblong shape and white sugar coating reminds them of the Christ child wrapped in a white blanket.

Stollen originated in the city of Dresden in the early 1400s. Because the cakes are loaded with fruit and nuts, they can be quite heavy. The heaviest stollen of all weighed almost 2 tons (1.8 metric tons). It measured about 26 feet (7.9m) long, 12 feet (3.4m) wide, 11 inches (30cm) thick. It was made in 1730 as a Christmas gift from a German king to his subjects. Ever since, a giant stollen is made in Dresden at Christmas as part of the Dresden Stollen Festival.

Modern stollens weigh about 4.5 pounds (2kg). But since many are custom-made, the weight varies. Many Germans bring their favorite ingredients to the local bakery, and the baker prepares the stollen using those ingredients. Besides dried fruit and nuts, stollen can be stuffed with marzipan, a paste made from almonds and sugar.

Germans eat stollen throughout the holiday season. It can be eaten hot or cold and spread with butter and jam. Amis, whose family is German, explains: "Every year my grandmother would make this for Christmas and we would have it for a light breakfast on Christmas morning.

A baker displays stollen, a heavy bread made with nuts and dried fruits.

. . . In my family, it's just not Christmas without . . . stollen."[19]

It is tempting to eat the whole cake. But because stollen keeps well, Germans usually save some for Easter.

Easter Chocolate

When Easter arrives, stollen is once again served. But it is chocolate that makes this holiday memorable. Easter baskets filled with chocolate eggs and chocolate bunnies have long been a tradition in Germany. This custom, also common in America, began in Germany.

Rabbits first became associated with Easter in the 1500s. A German story about an Easter rabbit that laid colored eggs inspired German children to leave their hats outside on Easter morning for the rabbit to use for its nest. The children's parents filled the hats with colored eggs. Eggs have always been a symbol of new life and this is why they appear at Easter. By the 1800s baskets had replaced the hats, and chocolate eggs and chocolate bunnies, both of which were invented in Germany, replaced the real ones.

Chocolate Bunny

Christmas Fudge

Making and eating fudge at Christmas is another popular German treat. You can substitute pecans for walnuts or chocolate-mint chips for the chocolate chips for a minty taste.

Ingredients:
18 ounces semisweet chocolate chips
1 14-ounce can sweetened condensed milk
pinch of salt
2 teaspoons vanilla extract
1 cup chopped walnuts

Instructions:
1. Put the chocolate chips, milk, and salt in a saucepan and cook over low heat until the chocolate is melted. Stir often.
2. Add the vanilla and nuts and stir.
3. Line an 8-inch square baking pan with nonstick foil. Pour the mixture into the pan.
4. Put the pan into the refrigerator and chill until the fudge becomes firm. Cut into small squares.

Makes about 50 squares.

Oktoberfest

Oktoberfest is a sixteen-day harvest festival held in Munich, Germany. It began in 1810 as an outdoor wedding for German king Ludwig I. The party was so much fun that it lasted for sixteen days, and the city of Munich has been throwing a similar party ever since.

Although Oktoberfest is associated with beer drinking, that is only a small part of the goings-on. Partygoers, of whom there are about 8 million a year, sit in huge tents and eat tons of grilled sausage, and thousands of roast chickens and pork knuckles. At the same time, a brass band plays. Merrymakers sing along and clap their hands to the music.

Hundreds of Germans gather under a huge tent to eat, drink, and celebrate Oktoberfest.

These early chocolate eggs and bunnies were made of solid chocolate because candy makers had not yet learned how to form hollow chocolate eggs. Today most German Easter chocolates are hollow. This makes them lighter tasting and easier to bite into. It also makes it possible to add fillings such as nuts, fruits, and marzipan.

Indeed, a modern German Easter basket is loaded with all kinds of chocolate treats. Even the lining of the basket can usually be eaten. Formed to look like a nest, it is made from sugar and water coated with dark chocolate. Resting on top are dozens of small milk chocolate eggs wrapped in gold foil or a giant bittersweet chocolate egg that may be more than 1 foot (30.48cm) long. Tucked beside the eggs you might find dark chocolate chicks, white chocolate bunnies, milk chocolate ladybugs, and sunny-side up eggs made from sugar, water, and chocolate.

No matter what fills the basket, German chocolate is made with the finest ingredients. Strict laws regulate its purity and ensure that plenty of cocoa butter, which gives the chocolate a rich, smooth taste, is used. Eating it, according to chocolate makers at Hachez, a popular German chocolate company, is "an entirely exceptional experience."[20]

Enjoying delectable treats like Easter chocolates, Christmas cookies, gingerbread, and stollen are indeed a wonderful experience. They make German holidays memorable and fun.

Metric Conversions

Mass (Weight)

1 ounce (oz.)	= 28.0 grams (g)
8 ounces	= 227.0 grams
1 pound (lb.) or 16 ounces	= 0.45 kilograms (kg)
2.2 pounds	= 1.0 kilogram

Liquid Volume

1 teaspoon (tsp.)	= 5.0 milliliters (ml)
1 tablespoon (tbsp.)	= 15.0 milliliters
1 fluid ounce (oz.)	= 30.0 milliliters
1 cup (c.)	= 240 milliliters
1 pint (pt.)	= 480 milliliters
1 quart (qt.)	= 0.96 liters (l)
1 gallon (gal.)	= 3.84 liters

Pan Sizes

8-inch cake pan	= 20 x 4-centimeter cake pan
9-inch cake pan	= 23 x 3.5-centimeter cake pan
11 x 7-inch baking pan	= 28 x 18-centimeter baking pan
13 x 9-inch baking pan	= 32.5 x 23-centimeter baking pan
9 x 5-inch loaf pan	= 23 x 13-centimeter loaf pan
2-quart casserole	= 2-liter casserole

Temperature

212° F	= 100° C (boiling point of wate
225° F	= 110° C
250° F	= 120° C
275° F	= 135° C
300° F	= 150° C
325° F	= 160° C
350° F	= 180° C
375° F	= 190° C
400° F	= 200° C

Length

1/4 inch (in.)	= 0.6 centimeter (cm)
1/2 inch	= 1.25 centimeters
1 inch	= 2.5 centimeters

Notes

Chapter 1: Three Important Ingredients

1. Maria Swaringen, *German Home Cooking.* Bloomington, IN: 1st Books, 2003, p. 106.

2. Marianna Olszewska Heberle, *German Cooking.* New York: HP Books, 1996, p. 120.

3. Katy Shaw Nelson, *The Eastern European Cookbook.* New York: Dover, 1973, p. 79.

4. Swaringen, *German Home Cooking,* p. 140.

5. Quoted in Mama's Kitchen, "German Potato Salad," www.in mamaskitchen.com/RECIPES/RECIPES/fruits_and_veggies. html/Germanpotatosal.html

Chapter 2: Satisfying Hearty Appetites

6. Helga Hughes, *Germany's Regional Recipes.* Iowa City, IA: Penfield, 1999, p. 24.

7. John, interview with the author in Las Cruces, NM, May 1, 2006.

8. German Embassy, "Sauerbraten with Potato Dumplings and Apple Sauce," www.germany.info/relaunch/culture/life/jan 97.html.

9. Olszewska Heberle, *German Cooking,* p. 87.

10. Janet Alexander, Recipe Zaar, "Roladen with Spaetzle," www. recipezaar.com/138674.

11. Swaringen, *German Home Cooking,* p. 157.

12. John T. Dickman, *Recipes and Reminiscence.* Bloomington, IN: 1st Books, 2001, p. 80

Chapter 3: Sandwiches and Sweets

13. Quoted in German Deli.com, "What I Miss About Germany," www.germandeli.com/whatdoyoumis.html.

14. Olszewska Heberle, *German Cooking*, p. 12.

15. Myra Waldo, *Seven Wonders of the Cooking World.* New York: Dodd, Mead, 1971, p. 196.

16. Quoted in Grandma's Marketplace, www.grandmasmarket place.com/custom.em?pid=336356.

Chapter 4: Holiday Treats

17. Quoted in Christmas Baking with Susie J, "Mother, Anna Ehrhardt's Springerle," www.christmas-baking.com/springerle 4.html.

18. Quoted in German Deli.com, "What I Miss About Germany," www.germandeli.com/whatdoyoumis.html.

19. Quoted in Recipezaar.com, "Amis's Christmas Stollen," www.recipezaar.com/recipe/getrecipe.zsp?id=141035.

20. Chocolat.com, "Hachez," www.chocolat.com/index.asp? PageAction=VIEWPROD&ProdID=157.

Black Forest cake: A multilayered chocolate and cherry cake.

brochen: The German word for "bakery rolls."

brotzeit: A mid-morning snack break in which bread is often eaten. *Brotzeit* means "bread time."

Charlemagne: Founding father and former emperor of Germany.

coffee klatsch: Get-together over coffee and cake.

cuisine: The food of a group of people or nation.

cure: To preserve meat or fish by smoking, drying, and/or salting it.

frankfurter: The German name for a hot dog.

kuchen: Single-layer cake.

lebkuchen: Gingerbread.

sauerbraten: A roast marinated in a sour sauce.

sauerkraut: Pickled, shredded cabbage.

schnitzel: A fried, breaded, boneless slice of veal, pork, or chicken.

spaetzle: Tiny egg noodles.

springerles: Sugar cookies made at Christmas time.

stollen: A Christmas cake similar to fruitcake.

torten: Layer cakes.

wiener schnitzel: Veal schnitzel.

weisswurst: A popular veal sausage, literally meaning "white sausage."

wurst: The German word for "sausage."

wurstmacher: Sausage maker.

for further Exploration

Books

Joan D'Amico, Karen Eich Drummond, *The Science Chef Travels Around the World.* New York: John Wiley & Sons, 1996. This book offers recipes from around the world, including Germany, with science experiments to go with the recipes.

Kathryn Lane, *Germany: The Culture.* New York: Crabtree, 2001. This book talks about German holidays, folktales, and music.

Sue Townsend, *Germany* (World of Recipes). Chicago: Heinemann, 2002. A German cookbook for kids.

Web Sites

A Taste of Germany (www.germanfoods.org): A Web site for adults that gives information about German foods, recipes, and links to German food stores in North America.

Germany for Kids (www.germanyinfo/relaunch/culture/life/G-kids/holidays.htm): This Web site maintained by the German embassy in Washington, D.C., gives information about German life, culture, holidays, and foods for kids.

History for Kids, "Ancient Germany," (www.history forkids.org/learn/germans/index.htm): This site explores ancient German history, including foods, art, architecture, with timelines and craft projects.

Index

Picture Credits

Cover: © Bob Krist/CORBIS

© Becky Luigart-Stayner/CORBIS, 38

Ben Fink /Jupiter Images, 20

Brian Hagiwara /Jupiter Images, 11, 12 (left)

Burke/Triolo/Jupiter Images, 40,46

Corinne Humphrey/Lonely Planet Images, 31

David Peevers/Lonely Planet Images, 39

E. Jane Armstrong/Jupiter Images, 19

© Envision/CORBIS, 35

Erik Rank/Jupiter Images, 6, 24

© George Steinmetz/CORBIS, 52

© Hans-Jprgen Wiedl/dpa/CORBIS, 44

Ionas Kaltenbach/Lonely Planet Images, 27

© Jan-Peter Kasper/dpa/CORBIS, 9

© Lee Snider/Photo Images/CORBIS, 33

Marc Berenson /Jupiter Images, 51

Mark Thomas /Jupiter Images, 15, 43

© Matthias Hiekel/epa/CORBIS, 49

© Michael S. Yamashita/CORBIS, 36

Monica Stevenson/Jupiter Images, 50

© Owen Franken/CORBIS, 21

© Peter Turnley/CORBIS, 30

Photos.com, 8, 14

Shimon & Tammar/Jupiter Images, 23

Steven Mark Needham/Jupiter Images, 12 (right)

Tamia Dowlatabadi, 5

About the Author

Barbara Sheen is the author of numerous books for young people. She lives in New Mexico with her family. In her spare time, she likes to swim, walk, garden, and read. And, of course, she loves to cook!